You Are Enough

 ❧❧❧❧ —————————

Is It Real Love or Your Need for Validation?
Overcoming People Pleasing and Emotionally
Unavailable Relationships

RAINIE HOWARD

Also by Rainie Howard:
ADDICTED TO PAIN
WHEN GOD SENT MY HUSBAND
UNDENIABLE BREAKTHROUGH
MIRACLES IN YOUR MOUTH

Rainie Howard Enterprises Publishing Agency
Saint Louis, MO 63108

For information about special discounts for bulk purchases or bringing the author
to your live event, please contact Rainie Howard Enterprises Sales
at 314-827-5216 or Contact@RainieHoward.com.
Manufactured in the United States of America
ISBN-10: 1-7340155-2-7
ISBN-13: 978-1-7340155-2-2

ACKNOWLEDGMENTS

I want to thank my wonderful and amazing husband, Patrick Howard. I love you so much. Special thanks to my children, Patrick Benjamin and Aniyah Howard. I love you with all my heart.

TABLE OF CONTENTS

INTRODUCTION

They tell you not to worry, be anxious, or be afraid, but what do you do when fear and anxiety were some of the first habits you learned as a child? What if, before you learned your ABC's or how to spell your name, you learned to be afraid of your dad? What if the person you learned to love was also the person you also learned to fear? What if your childhood included uncertainty, chaos, and instability? How do you stop being afraid of the uncertainties in life if fear and anxiety were some of the most major influences on your early development?

That was my life. Before age five, I had experienced the tumultuous effects of a toxic relationship. I can still envision my mother's small apartment, where it all took place. I can still hear the loud arguing and fighting and the sounds of the police coming after all the chaos. My father was very unstable. He struggled with drug abuse and was very possessive of my mom. Whenever they broke up, he became very jealous and paranoid that someone else would take his place. I can remember him breaking into our home in the middle of the night. He climbed through our bedroom window, suspiciously trying to catch my mom with someone else. Although I was afraid of my dad, I also loved him deeply. He made me feel like the most valuable, beautiful princess in the world. How can you have so much love for someone and yet be fearful of them?

One day, my family had a backyard BBQ party, and everyone was there, my cousins, aunts, uncles and grandmother. My mom's new boyfriend Larry was there too. As I was playing with the other kids in the yard, I heard someone call my name. When I looked up, I saw that it was my dad, hiding in a bush. I ran over to him, and he asked me to point out which man was my mom's boyfriend. I pointed to Larry, and a few minutes later, my dad ruined the party by starting a fight with Larry. Someone called the police to break it up, and my mom was upset with me for telling my dad who Larry was.

I was only four years old. I couldn't understand how I was wrong. But I learned that my words could cause trouble, and I felt like it was all my fault. That taught me to keep quiet, not to speak much to adults or people I didn't know well, and to always try to please others and gain their approval. I became a people-pleaser. I learned that the intentions behind my words didn't matter. I learned that I was a troublemaker, but I was determined to do my best to try to be good. I was ashamed of my dad's bad actions, and I took that shame on myself. My dad's struggle with drug abuse and his time in prison caused me great shame and embarrassment, and I internalized those feelings as well.

I can't remember ever feeling like I was good enough. At age six, I became very responsible. I began cleaning my mom's entire house and staying home by myself until my mom got off of work so I could help take care of my little sister. I wanted to make my mom happy, but I didn't know then that it was impossible to make anyone happy. When I made mistakes and got in trouble, instead of learning from the situation and forgiving myself, I would become guilty and ashamed. I would say to myself, "You are bad. You can't do nothing right." Those thoughts would influence me to work even harder to be "good" or even perfect and to make others happy. But no matter how hard I worked, it was never enough. The guilt and shame consumed me.

It became difficult to say no. I could never say no, no matter what was asked of me. Even if I didn't want to give something away, I could not say no when it was asked of me. I remember getting in trouble for going through the refrigerator and giving strawberries to the kids outside. I would give all my toys away because I wanted to please people. I wanted to make people happy. I didn't like it when people were mad at me, especially my mother. I lived to please her. The shame and toxic reputation of my dad drove me to strive for perfection and often left me feeling like a failure, confused as to why I couldn't be perfect.

I was quiet and shy in school, and I would do everything in my strength to make good grades and have excellent behavior. In first grade, I received my very first report card. It was sealed in an envelope, and my teacher told me to give it to my mother. I was so nervous. I dreaded bad news. I knew I didn't do anything to get in trouble or get bad grades, but I worried it would say something like that inside anyway, and I feared my mom being angry with me. I gave my mom the envelope. She opened it and read the card inside. To my surprise, she was happy. She was proud of my accomplishments. She said that I had a great report card, and I felt relieved and happy. I was mainly happy because of my mom's reaction, not because of my own successes. My mom never heard of any problems with me in school. I always wanted to gain her approval, and school was an easy way to do so.

As I grew into a young adult, the roots of fear, anxiety, guilt and shame inside of me led me to become a shy, professional people-pleaser and perfectionist. I lacked inner peace and joy, because my happiness depended on how I made others feel. The more I strived to please people and make others happy, the more I felt like a failure. I had to free myself from the pressures of pleasing others and focus more on getting in touch with the Holy Spirit and God's calling for my life. I had to no longer view myself as a failure but to see myself the way God sees me. I had to understand that old things have passed away and that I'm a new creature. I am more than a conqueror. I had to change my view of myself.

You may not have experienced an abusive dad or demanding mom, but maybe you can relate to feeling anxious and fearful. Maybe you've struggled with being a people-pleaser due to a fear of rejection. Many of these habits can lead to emotionally unavailable relationships. These develop when you attract users and people who only want to be with you when it's convenient. These people aren't committed to you and benefit from your need to be accepted. They profit from your fear of loneliness. They get away with mistreating you because of your personal guilt and shame. Deep down inside, you don't believe you're worthy of true love. You struggle with the idea of being good enough for love.

This book is going to transform your entire life. You will create new habits that will give you peace in your mind and joy in your heart. You will build the strength to completely let go of toxic relationships and the confidence and self-esteem to grow in healthy relationships. You may feel like you're not strong enough, pretty enough, or smart enough, but you will learn that in our weaknesses, God is made strong. God has given you everything you need to fulfill your destiny. Never doubt what God is doing in you. You must understand that you are enough.

"The Lord is my shepherd. I lack nothing." –Psalm 23:1

Trust the process. Complete this entire book and start your journey to an empowered, happy, healthy life.

CHAPTER 1

LOSING YOURSELF

In the beginning, he wouldn't stop pursuing me. He texted me hourly, sometimes ten times a day. He told me everything I wanted to hear and more. He said he'd always dreamt of being with someone as beautiful as me. He always wanted to be with me from morning to night. He said he had secretly had a crush on me for a long time. Although I didn't show him any interest, he wouldn't give up on winning my heart. It was like he couldn't get enough of me.

At first, I tried very hard to protect my heart and not get too involved. Steve was a very attractive man, the kind of man most women desired. He had the cutest eyes and an athletic body. I already had a strong physical attraction for him, but I was very guarded, because he was known to be a player. He had a reputation for cheating. I told him several times that I couldn't get involved with him because of his ways. He would say, "Brittany, I would never cheat on you! You are different from any other girl I've ever been with. If I had ever been with you, I'd have treated you like the queen you are."

I fell for it. I wanted to believe him, so I decided to trust him and maybe, one day, give him my heart. I only did so because he made me feel so wanted and desired, and it had been a long time since I'd felt those feelings. He made me feel so loved. I had been single for a long time, and I didn't realize how much I longed for love and companionship. Once we were together, he continued to pursue my heart daily. He sent love messages, took me on romantic dates, surprised me with flowers at work, and told me that he envisioned starting a family with me one day. I finally gave in and opened my heart to Steve. I started to really trust him, so I gave him all of me, my mind, body and soul. My entire life revolved around Steve. It's like I started living for him. If I went anywhere besides work, it was because Steve asked me to go. If I cooked a new meal, it was because Steve wanted to eat it. I couldn't get him off my mind. I daydreamed about every little moment with him.

Everything was going great until one day it all stopped. It's like he woke up and no longer had interest in me. I stopped getting the calls, text messages, and quality time. No more love notes, no more "just because" flowers and no more date nights. He became too busy for me. There were times when I didn't hear from him for weeks. I would call him, and he wouldn't answer my call. I left messages, and he still wouldn't call me back. I was confused. When I finally did get to talk to him, he gave me a million excuses as to why he hadn't made time for me. I believed him, because I wanted to make our love work.

Now, whenever he came around, it was only late at night, and he only wanted to come to my house. We no longer went out on dates or spent time at his house. I would suggest that we go to his house sometimes, but he always had an excuse about his roommate and why it wasn't a good idea. We developed a pattern in our relationship. We only saw each other about twice a month, and it was always at my house in the late-night hours. Although I missed how close we used to be, I settled for the short moments he gave me, because I felt like it was better than nothing. Plus, Steve had issues with my family. My mom told me that I deserved someone better than Steve. She said he was very unpredictable, and she didn't believe he was mature enough for a committed relationship with me. I didn't want my family to know I was still in a relationship with Steve, so it was best that we kept things the way they were for that reason.

One morning, while I was making coffee in the break room at work, I overheard some coworkers congratulating our intern on her pregnancy. I went over to congratulate her too, and I asked her how far along she was. "Thanks, Brittany! I'm three months," she said. Another coworker said, "I'm sure Steve is very excited to be a soon-to-be dad." Jamie blushed and started smiling. She said, "Yes, he is. He took these pictures holding the ultrasound of the baby." As she opened her phone to show everyone the pictures, every nerve in my body started to vibrate. My hands got sweaty, and I felt a rush of panic brush through my body. I looked at her phone, and sure enough, it was Steve. It was my Steve, the man I had given my entire life to. It was the man I had given my heart, mind, body and soul to. It was the man I had made all my future plans with. It was the man I had grown to fall in love with. My Steve was going to be the father of Jamie's baby. My Steve had been in a completely different relationship all this time.

I couldn't do anything but run to the bathroom. I sat in the

3

stall and cried like a baby. I couldn't stop crying. I had chest pain, my head started to hurt and all I could do was weep. I cried until all my tears completely washed all the makeup off my face. My eyes were swollen and bloodshot red. I didn't say anything to anyone the entire day. I went home and laid in my bed and cried for the rest of the night too. I felt humiliated, and I didn't have anyone to talk to about it, because no one knew that I was still in a relationship with Steve. I was ashamed. I had a reputation of being a strong confident woman, and no one knew I allowed Steve to come and go as he pleased. I often spoke badly about women like that. As much as I frowned at side-chicks and mistresses, I had never expected to become one. I had to face the reality that I wasn't Steve's main girl. He had been playing me. The reason I could never spend time with him at his house is because Jamie lived there with him. The reason we could no longer go out on dates is because his relationship with Jamie was known all over town. It was only a secret to me.

Steve called me a week later, saying that he missed me and wanted to come and see me. I told him that I knew about Jamie and the baby and that I didn't want to ever see him again. To my surprise, he broke down and started crying. He said he loved me and never wanted to lose me. He told me he didn't love Jamie the way he loved me. He said he didn't want the baby and that Jamie set him up. He said he planned to leave her to be with me, but because of the pregnancy he had to wait. I cried and asked him how he could hurt me so badly. He begged for my forgiveness and drove to my house to make up. I let him in and received every word he said and cried on his shoulder as he held me. We made up that night, and I felt a temporary relief from the pain. I was entangled in a love triangle, and I willingly went along with it only because I couldn't imagine my life without Steve. The pain of not having him in my life seemed unbearable, and I was willing to do whatever it took not to suffer alone. I never said a word to Jamie, and I allowed Steve to visit me twice a month. I figured it was better than being alone. I became numb to the hurt and pain. I was trapped in an emotionally unavailable relationship, and I didn't know how to get out.

Paralyzed by the Fear of Loneliness

Brittany is just like many single women who desire love, companionship and commitment in a relationship. However, her insecurities, low self-esteem and fear of loneliness have led her to continue a toxic relationship with a man who isn't faithful to her. This is where things get tricky, because Brittany knows and understands that she deserves better, but she's stuck. The fear of loneliness and the fear of pain from a breakup has paralyzed her from ending the relationship she has with Steve. Plus, she doesn't believe she will ever find true love. Brittany has numbed herself to the pain of Steve and Jamie's relationship. She has lost her passion and desire for true love. She is living in the fantasy of her old love with Steve, and her past experiences of joy and excitement consume her mind and keep her trapped in an emotionally unavailable relationship.

Why do people settle for emotionally unavailable relationships? It's difficult to walk away from the lies, it's hard to walk away from the deception and it's complicated to walk away from the pain. Don't be fooled by the toxic love of an unavailable relationship, because it can feel like real love. But toxic relationships are dead-end relationships. They are relationships that never prosper. They struggle to elevate in life, but they never truly do. They make us feel happy some of the time and make us miserable most of the time. This is usually because your partner fulfills a very strong basic need in you, like acceptance or attention, and you become addicted and dependent on that partner for fulfilling that need. You unconsciously ignore the fact that your partner cannot or will not fulfill the other long-term needs of a healthy relationship.

Entangled in Deception and Lies

Have you ever wondered how some women stay in relationships with men who aren't fully available? Have you done this? You may be attracting men who are detached and unavailable most of the time. He contacts you whenever it's convenient or only weekly instead of daily. However, when he is available, he tells you everything you need to hear. He gives you an emotional, physical and mental fill up. He knows exactly what you want to hear, and he pays close attention to what it takes to get a reaction from you. He can be very sweet but there's something that's just not right. He knows how to give you just enough attention to keep you. The fill-up is small compared to the large distance of separation within the relationship, but you take this small amount of attention he gives you and hold onto it in your mind as a major thing.

Really, he's using you for whenever he's available. "Mr. Nice and sweet but just not right" is who you're dealing with. You have become entangled in his lies, deception and game. Yes, it's his game, because he's been playing you. He has figured out exactly what its takes to win your heart and now he has you. He plays these games in order to keep you while he benefits in ways that hurt you. If he knows you're insecure, he will exploit that weakness by comparing you to other women, and when you call him out on it, he will act like you're overreacting. He knows how to make you question yourself and even blame yourself for his bad behavior. Then he punishes you by disappearing. He will stop answering your calls, he will ignore your text messages and he will pretend that every argument is all your fault just to manipulate and control the situation. You may not even realize you're being played like this, because manipulation is deceiving.

It's important that you understand that manipulators are very skillful in listening to your every word and finding out all your weaknesses in order to use them against you. You can protect yourself by maintaining confidence. Your confidence should specifically be in your standards. Having the skill to confidently socialize and showing confidence in body language will only go so far if you still allow a man to have his way with your time, body and emotions. You should never compromise your values and standards just to please someone else. The moment he stops communicating with you and being transparent and honest, that's when it's time to withdraw. As painful as breaking up may be, it cannot compare to the pain of losing yourself. As painful as loneliness may be, it cannot compare to the pain of low self-esteem and a lack of self-respect. It's important that you guard your heart and protect your peace. Your dignity, your legacy and your purpose is what you are fighting for. No man can give you that. It's only something you can give yourself.

Understand that unavailable relationships aren't just relationships that involve infidelity. They may include the marriage of a husband and wife who are too consumed and too busy with life's demands to add value to their relationship or an on-again off-again relationship that lacks the deep companionship of intimate communication. They aren't even all romantic relationships. Unavailable relationships can be between relatives, friends, co-workers and romantically involved couples. Breaking up a marriage or refusing to see a friend again isn't the answer for every unavailable relationship. There are also simpler, practical actions you can apply in your current relationship to stop allowing mistreatment, abuse and neglect.

You may feel like you have lost yourself in an unavailable relationship, but by the time you finish this book, you will have found yourself and even more. The purpose of this book is not to convince you to eliminate your relationship but to give you the guidance and support to enjoy healthier relationships. You will receive some actionable strategies to help you create boundaries and protect your peace and purpose. You will learn to say no without losing yourself. Let's get to the root of why you are feeling not good enough and why you may be attracting emotionally unavailable relationships.

Affirmations

Say the following affirmations out loud.

- I am loved.
- I will not settle for less than God's best.
- I am strong and confident.
- I believe in true love.

Take Action

What have you been avoiding in your life that has caused you to deny the truth about a relationship you have?

_____

_____

_____

_____

_____

Have you been living in a fantasy of what *was* while ignoring the truth about what *is?*

_____

_____

_____

_____

_____

How have you been manipulated in the past?

_____

_____

_____

What are the emotionally unavailable relationships in your life?

_____

_____

_____

_____

CHAPTER 2

—————— ❧❧❧❧ ——————

TRUE IDENTITY

The relationship you have with yourself will impact every relationship you have with others. As we consider the reasons that you are attracting unavailable relationships, we must first analyze what's going on in your mind, spirit and soul before you even enter a relationship. What are your beliefs, values and goals?

Let's consider Brittany's situation. She had been single for four years before Steve came along. She secretly struggled with the belief that she would never get married and would always be alone. She also had a negative self-image. She didn't like her body size and struggled to lose weight. She didn't have a healthy self-esteem, and she struggled to discover her life's purpose. She often thought negatively about her life and accomplishments. She never felt like she would be good enough to live the kind of life she envied in others. She desired a relationship, but her fear of rejection prevented her from actively pursuing one.

Just like many single women, Brittany was waiting to be rescued by a man. In her mind, her life was boring and unfulfilling. She spent most of her time working or lounging around at home. She didn't have any dreams, goals or future plans. She lived day by day, unsure of what she really wanted in life. When Steve came into her life, she was empty and void of so much that it was easy for him to give her some of the things she neglected to give herself. He pursued her, showing that he saw her as valuable, and took time to listen and get to know her. Before, Brittany hadn't even had the desire to pursue or get to know herself. Steve sent her love messages, planned romantic dates and bought her gifts to show his appreciation of her. Brittany had never done anything nice for herself. She had never written words of affirmation or positive messages to encourage herself when she felt sad or depressed, and she would have saw it as weird to plan a date by herself or buy gifts for herself. She didn't think any of it was necessary. Steve even talked to Brittany about the future he envisioned having with her. Brittany had never envisioned much for her future. She had never had any idea what kind of future life she wanted. She was lost.

It's easy to understand how Brittany could latch on desperately to everything Steve gave her and, in return, give him her mind, body and soul. When she did this, she left nothing for herself, and when Steve stopped pursuing her and giving her everything she lacked, he was only treating her the way she had always treated herself. The important thing to understand about this example is that Brittany had attracted the same love, acceptance and attention that she gave herself, and that was what led her to an emotionally unavailable relationship.

The following is an excerpt from my book, *Addicted to Pain: Renew Your Mind and Heal Your Spirit From a Toxic Relationship in 30 Days.*

"There are physical, mental and spiritual characteristics of an emotional pain addict. Some call it toxic love addiction.

Here's a few signs that your relationship is toxic and it's time to move on:

- You are living in past memories more than present experiences.
- You keep justifying your partner's bad actions.
- Your relationship brings more pain than joy.
- Your partner is causing you emotional, physical or verbal pain.
- Your values and beliefs are different from those of your partner.
- You stay in the relationship because you expect things to get better.
- Your partner puts little to no effort into the relationship.
- The relationship holds you back and prevents both of you from growing as individuals.

If you are attracting the same type of toxic relationship with different people, or if you can't seem to heal after a breakup but instead continue to hold tight to a relationship that should have ended a long time ago, this book was written specifically for you.

You may be thinking, 'But he's a good man. He just has a few issues. Plus, I don't want to be lonely. He apologized, and I think we can work through it. I need him. He helps with the kids and pays the bills, and I don't know what I would do by myself. I'm not addicted to pain. I just love him, and I refuse to accept that he doesn't love me.'

I'm going to be completely honest with you. Everything you've been telling yourself is the reason are stuck. I'm going to help you love and respect yourself enough to walk away from anyone or anything that does not lead you to a closer relationship with God and help you grow mentally and spiritually. As you move on and heal from this relationship, I'm going to help you turn this hurtful loss into the best thing that ever happened to you."

You Attract What's in You

How can you expect to receive something you're not willing to give? Your response may be, "But I give my partner love, affection, attention and acceptance!" But that is not what I am talking about. It is when you don't give these things to *yourself* that you teach them to treat you badly. After your partner has gotten to know you, he will began to figure out that your standards are lower than he assumed and that all those things he did in the beginning to win your heart weren't really required.

Don't get me wrong. I'm not saying that Steve had a right to cheat and mistreat Brittany. What I am saying is that you attract what you unconsciously communicate from what's inside your mind and soul. This is true even if you have a reputation for being a powerful, strong and intelligent person. Your outward appearance displays confidence and strength, but your inward soul may still communicate insecurity and weakness. Your powerful reputation is a persona. It's the role you play every day when you go out into the world, but as you develop true, intimate relationships, the reality of your truth is revealed. The reason you attract unavailable, loveless relationships is because you struggle to accept and give yourself the attention you desperately need. The acceptance and even the toxic love that comes from an emotionally unavailable partner is satisfying because it fills your void of self-love.

This is why Brittany is willing to settle for a love triangle with Steve and Jamie. Steve is still treating Brittany better than she treats herself, and a relationship with only herself is desperately lonely. She can't bare to go through the boredom and unfulfillment of being alone. If the relationship that she have with herself was full of substance and strength, ending the toxic relationship would be a piece of cake for her. As a matter of fact, if you thrive in a healthy relationship with yourself, you won't even tolerate the warning signs of a toxic relationship.

Your Fears are Keeping You Alone

Maybe you're nothing like Brittany. You may be attracting unavailable relationships in a different way. You may be very social and outgoing. On the outside, you appear to be spontaneous, fun and ready for love, and you think you are. You have been seeking love for a long time, and you can't understand why you keep attracting unfit partners who can't support you the way you desire. You are confused about why you can't seem to find "the one." You may be in denial that you are really emotionally unavailable yourself.

Deep down inside, you may not want one person to have so much of you. You enjoy your life, and you don't want to lose yourself in a relationship. You fear the unknown. You may also fear the devastation of ended love, because in your past experience, love has often come with pain. These fears are keeping you alone and single. You may have some unfinished grief and healing to deal with, and you may have been avoiding it because it's so painful to consider, but your healing is required for you to move forward. Life has a way of confronting you with everything you try to avoid. It comes to you in different ways. You have to eventually deal with it. It takes great courage to give and receive love, and although on the outside, you show a desire to be in a loving relationship, on the inside, you fear love.

It's easy to focus much of your attention on your emotionally unavailable partner, but have you ever considered that the reason you attract unavailable relationships is because you're unavailable? Yes, I said it. You are unavailable. You may be thinking, "No, I'm available. My heart is open. I want love and connection. I'm available and ready for a relationship."

You may be saying that with your mouth, but what are you saying unconsciously with your mind and heart? Most people who attract unavailable relationships are indeed unconsciously unavailable. Many of them have a fear of never finding real love. They have negative thoughts about their potential to find someone who will really love and accept the real them. They are so insecure about their weaknesses and past failures that they unconsciously believe no one will ever love their truth. They are ashamed of their hidden faults and fear rejection when their weaknesses are discovered. These people often want a relationship, but they are afraid of true intimacy.

Sometimes, these fears even lead people to feel that an

unavailable relationship works perfectly. They don't want to be smothered. They enjoy partners who are distant and give appropriate space. They are comfortable in long-distance relationships and prefer partners who travel a lot. They may even prefer partners who are in other committed relationships. Maybe you've wondered why some people become involved with a partner who is married. These people may unconsciously prefer that kind of situation because the detachment helps to ease their fear of being smothered or losing themselves to a relationship. Some women are attracted to married men because of the safety of never really having anything to lose.

This kind of thinking can grow out of experiences and beliefs from your childhood or from a failure to properly heal from the loss of a past relationship. The fear of losing another person you love or even losing yourself will lead you to settle for an unavailable relationship. You are settling, because deep down inside you are trying to protect yourself. You are protecting yourself from intimacy. You are afraid to unveil your truth, and this part of your relationship has nothing to do with your partner.

The answer to this is in truly learning to love and forgive yourself. That's where you'll find healing. That's where you can begin to have healthy relationships. It starts with you, with understanding that you are enough. Your weaknesses, your flaws, your mistakes and your failures do not define you. You can learn to accept them, forgive yourself and grow in love with yourself and others. If you commit yourself to completing the necessary work of self-acceptance and self-love, you can heal, walk in boldness and confidently love freely again. You will be able to do this without fear, because your new wisdom and daily habits will support a healthier lifestyle.

Maybe you struggle with knowing your purpose or understanding what you really want in life. It's very common for both women and men to feel confused about what they truly desire. If you never stop to take the time to do the inner work that you need to do to know and understand who God created you to be, you will never understand what it means to fulfill your purpose and walk in your truth. Many of us desire abundant blessings and God's favor, but we aren't willing to do what it takes to earn these experiences. It requires change. You must be willing to change your mindset and daily habits. You can't continue to think negative thoughts and fill your time with toxic conversations, bad news and the unimportant distractions of media, internet and entertainment and expect positive transformation in your life. You must be willing to change from the inside out.

Many of us experience emotionally unavailable relationships in our marriages as well. Some married couples function as two single people. Marriages become lifeless and dry, because couples stop nurturing their relationships after their weddings. Our culture puts more emphasis on dating, engagements and weddings, as if that's all couples have to look forward to. Marriages are failing because there aren't many examples of how to experience love, passion and lifetime commitment in a strong marriage. Marriages are left trying to survive in a spiritual desert void of emotions. Couples are left secretly wondering whether they made the right decision to marry and eventually regretting their union. It's a tragedy, but thank God that there is hope. Relationships can heal and be restored.

My first question to you in helping you change the quality of your relationships is, how do you treat yourself? Do you speak positive affirmations over your life daily? Do you nurture your mind, body and soul through meditation, prayer, healthy eating and daily relaxation? Do you live a full life by consistently learning new things, passionately accomplishing new goals and utilizing your gifts and talents? If you answered no to any of those questions, I want you to know there's hope and that you can start living a more fulfilled life starting today. It's never too late, and the good news is you don't need anything or anyone but God to start. No matter what situation you're in right now, God will strengthen you to overcome.

Healing always starts with forgiveness. Forgiveness is not about condoning wrongdoings or forgetting that bad things have happened. You may remember what happened and remain totally against the act of another, but when you let go of your resentment and your pursuit of revenge toward that person, you are operating in forgiveness. Sometimes you won't receive an apology, and you may never get the closure you desire, but you must still be willing to forgive. Forgiveness is consciously letting go of resentment and vengeance, whether the people who wronged you deserve them or not.

Whether you are forgiving yourself or another person, there are numerous mental, spiritual and physical blessings that you receive in your life when you choose to forgive. According to a study in the *Journal of Behavioral Medicine*, people who only forgive when they have received an apology die earlier than people who forgive unconditionally, with or without an apology. Forgiveness will decrease your stress, help you sleep better, increase your energy and strengthen your peace of mind. It's important that you understand that it all starts with you. Let's go deeper.

Affirmations

Say the following affirmations out loud.

- I am good enough.
- My life is exciting and fulfilling.
- I love and forgive myself.
- I am not ashamed of my past.
- I am not defined by my past.
- I forgive those who hurt me.

Take Action

What are your beliefs, values and goals?

_____

_____

_____

_____

_____

In what area of your life have you been waiting to be rescued?

_____

_____

_____

_____

_____

What have you been neglecting to give yourself?

_____

_____

_____

What do you envision for your life?

_____

_____

_____

_____

How can you give yourself the love, acceptance and attention you desire?

_____

_____

_____

_____

Are your fears keeping you single?

_____

_____

_____

_____

How do you treat yourself daily?

_____

_____

_____

_____

Who do you need to forgive, and how will you forgive them, with or without closure?

_____

_____

_____

_____

_____

_____

_____

_____

CHAPTER 3

—————— ❧❦ ——————

EXPOSED DECEPTION

Understand this: what you focus on is what you attract. What you believe is what you receive. This is true whether your primary focus is positive or negative. If your mind is filled with thoughts about how you don't want any more toxic relationships or you refuse to fall in love with a cheater again, don't be surprised if you start another toxic relationship with a cheater. You aren't going to attract that type of relationship because you want it. You attract it because it's what you've been focused on. Have you ever heard someone say, "The very thing I feared the most became my reality?" When your primary focus is a negative thing, something you don't want, it is what you will attract. You manifest what you fill your mind with.

"Just as he thinks in his heart, so is he…" –Proverbs 23:7

You become what's in your mind. You manifest the meditations of your heart. What you replay in your mind over and over again becomes your reality, whether you are replaying what you don't want or what you do. It's your choice what to focus on. You choose what you want to think. We are not what we say or what we do. We are what we think.

Listen to your mind. Have you ever paid close attention to your thoughts? One day I listened closely to my thoughts, and I discovered how anxious, insecure and negative my thoughts were. I was often worried about what people thought of me and how I looked in my clothes and whether or not I could gain people's approval. I was a mess. I was often disappointed in myself because I wasn't losing the extra weight I gained. I compared myself to others and was never satisfied. I discovered how hard I was on myself and how much being a perfectionist caused me anxiety and fear. I had to change my thoughts before I started experiencing God's peace and love in my life. I had to forgive others and myself by meditating on scriptures that reinforced God's purpose for my life. I had to detox from the toxic thoughts and negative beliefs before I saw total transformation in my life, but when I did, I grew to accept all of me, my weakness and strengths, my failures and accomplishments.

"Do not conform to the pattern of this world, but be transformed by the renewing of your mind. Then you will be able to test and approve what God's will is—his good, pleasing and perfect will." –Romans 12:2

There is a pattern of negative thinking in this world. You can see and hear it through the news, other media and entertainment outlets. People are drawn to negative news. Negativity and drama sells. This is one of the main reasons I personally avoid watching the daily news. There have been times when I'd hear about a devastating story of homicide and my mind would start replaying the story of the person who committed the crime, going over and over the incident with questions. Why would he do it? What was his motive? What was going on in his mind? The thoughts became obsessive as I tried to comprehend, and I could not get the story out of my head. We can easily conform to the negative patterns of this world, but the Bible recommends instead that we be transformed by the renewal of our minds. You can renew your mind by letting go of negative thoughts and carefully choosing what you want to replace them with, and your new thoughts will transform your life.

We attract negative relationships because we often have negative and toxic internal beliefs about ourselves hidden in our subconscious minds, and these beliefs are validated by the toxic relationships we experience. You may have a positive personality and friendly attitude, so no one understands why you keep finding yourself in negative relationships. Your positive attitude may be your persona, the role you play and the mask you wear for the world, but the real you is hidden. It's hidden deep in your subconscious mind, and it is still hurt by past experiences that left you believing you weren't good enough. The root of that core belief keeps attracting relationships and situations that confirm the belief that you aren't good enough. Your experiences and relationships will change when your expectations change, your expectations will change when your beliefs change, and your beliefs will change when your daily thoughts change.

Your Personality Strengths may be Attracting Toxic People
Your strongest positive character traits may become the weaknesses that attracts toxic people. For example, my strong attributes are my ability to be genuine with people and show

compassion to them. I love helping people and being accommodating. Unfortunately, those positive traits can become weaknesses in toxic relationships. My genuine compassion and helpful, accommodating personality can easily become obsessive people-pleasing. Toxic people who are pushy and demanding often take advantage of my traits, and my tendency is to respond by trying to appease them so they won't get mad at me. I used to try to convince them that I'm nice and they should like me by answering all their calls, rarely saying no and losing myself in the process. I had to learn how to create boundaries and become more aware of how people use my strengths for their personal gain. Notice that I didn't say that I changed my positive traits. I'm still compassionate, genuine and helpful to others, but now, I'm more aware of how toxic people will try to take advantage of those facts.

The following are positive attributes you should be aware of that may be attracting toxic people, along with tips to help you take action and prevent these people from taking advantage of you and having a negative impact on your life.

1. **You're overly generous with your quality time and listening ear.** Toxic people cling to generous people who are willing to drop everything and give them their time. The more you fulfill their requests for your time, the more they ask for it. You find yourself resentful, because after they're gone, your time feels like it has been wasted. Your time spent on them isn't productive, because it is spent focused *only* on them, and they pay you no attention in return. They talk about what they

want to talk about, and your only purpose is to listen. It's not easy finding a good listener, so when they find one in you, they will talk for hours. They ignore your body language and any verbal clues you give them that they are asking too much of you, because they are focused on how they want to be heard. They share negative, unsolicited details about their life because they need a listening ear to dump all their toxic trash in.

Prevention: Before you enter into a conversation with a person like this, determine how much time you're willing to spend with them. Be sure to limit your conversation with toxic people to only a few minutes. It's very important that you become aware of your feelings and needs and put them first in conversations with people like this. Generous people often give with no limits, but it's important that you don't allow people to drain you of all that you have. Giving all your energy, time and attention to a person will cause poverty in your mental creativity and poverty in productive time. When you say "no" to these toxic people and limit your time with them, you will preserve yourself for the people and plans that elevate you for greatness.

2. **You're transparent and openly share your dreams.** Toxic people often settle in life. Many of them don't strive to accomplish dreams and set goals but they may be interested in your pursuit of them. We've all heard

the saying that "opposites attract," and the saying is true for toxic people like this, who are often attracted to positive people. Your transparency in sharing your vision, dreams and goals is what they like about you, but they may begin to use it against you. Their fear that you will succeed and leave them may cause them to plant negative thoughts or doubts in your mind to convince you to settle in life like them. They are afraid of losing you, and their solution to that problem is to discourage your dreams and goals.

Prevention: Do not share your dreams and goals with toxic people. Although you may be transparent and open, not everyone should have the privilege of knowing your dreams and aspirations. Surround yourself with like-minded, positive people who are accomplishing and pursuing their own dreams and goals, and share your future plans with those people.

3. **You are a loyal peacemaker.** Peacemakers are willing to do whatever it takes to keep the peace, create mutual agreement and promote cooperation. However, some toxic people find excitement and pleasure in drama, and they actively work to dismantle the peace while you work to maintain it. They may say they want a healthy relationship with you, but if they always start fights and leave it up to you to put the pieces back together. You always find yourself walking on eggshells around them, and they, on the other hand, don't mind upsetting you,

While you are stressing yourself out, trying to build a bridge in a relationship, the other person is trying just as hard to destroy the bridge as you build it.

Prevention: Sometimes closure and mutual agreement with toxic people are not worth maintaining. Are you trying to build something that's going nowhere? Some bridges are meant to crumble, and some relationships aren't meant to be fixed. It's important that you understand that you can't change people, even people who say they want to change. People may tell you what they believe you want to hear, but they show you the truth in their actions. If they aren't actively trying to contribute to their relationship with you, you need to stop doing all of the work yourself. If they aren't working toward peace, you cannot be peaceful enough for both of you. You can only control yourself. Save yourself the time and energy, let go and let God.

4. **You are very optimistic about people and tend to ignore their negative warning signs and traits.** Maya Angelou said, "When people show you who they are, believe them the first time." We often ignore negative behaviors of toxic people because we expect them to change. We are willing to live in the fantasy in our minds than to face the reality of the truth of a toxic relationship. We brush off their put-downs and ignore their lies until we actually become accustomed to and even comfortable with their bad behaviors and we have

to make excuses about the reasons we keep them around.

Prevention: Never second-guess your discomfort with someone or your intuition about them. Our bodies respond to physical injury by giving us physical pain in order to prevent further injury, and in the same way, we experience emotional discomfort or pain to prevent the emotional injuries of toxic environments. Don't ignore the warning signs.

It's important to understand the state of mind you're most often in, know your weaknesses and strengths and recognize how they can be used and abused in relationships with others.

A Friend to Your Pain and an Enemy to Your Purpose

Sometimes, toxic relationships aren't as obvious as the ones listed above. Several years ago, I was really busy with my nonprofit organization Sisters of Hope, and I was seeking volunteers who were available to help me with operations and programming. During this season of my life, I struggled with a strong need for recognition and appreciation, and I desired affirmation by others. Around this time, I met Jessica, a young woman who was very helpful and excited to volunteer. She helped with programming, setting up classes and serving the youth. Although she had some toxic personality traits ,such as being pushy, controlling and possessive, I ignored them because she gave so much of her time and she often affirmed me with flattering affirmations. I knew that Jessica herself was unhappy in her life. She often talked about her past and the toxic experiences she encountered.

Unhappy people cling to easygoing, positive people and often mistakenly believe they can find their happiness in others. They may be overly generous with flattery and gifts, doing everything they can to please you, as long as you say yes to their every request in return. They need you to answer all their phone calls, spend as much time with them as they desire and be there for them whenever they need you, filling them up where they are empty.

Jessica's possessiveness and controlling ways became worse throughout the years. She often showed signs of jealousy and envy towards other friends of mine and even resented my husband at times. I was often confused about our relationship, because there was a mixture of positive and negative attributes. I gave her a listening ear, positive advice and availability. She often volunteered to help without me asking, and she affirmed my achievements. My insecurities and need for flattery enjoyed having her around, but her toxic behaviors were detrimental to my spiritual growth. She was a friend to my pain and an enemy to my purpose. My brokenness connected us, but my destiny divided us. It took me years to finally realize my relationship with Jessica was not healthy. It wasn't a true, genuine friendship, and I realized it needed to end.

My relationship with Jessica was blocking my breakthrough. I needed to be delivered from my insecurities, doubts and fears. My deliverance was going to remain on hold as long as I allowed her to feed my ego. I needed to break free and go to God. I realized our friendship could have survived if she was willing to go through her own deliverance of freeing herself as well, and I discussed it with her, but she didn't want to heal her toxic ways. Her mouth said she did, but she actions showed she didn't. I prayed for months about our relationship, and finally, one day, her toxic behavior got to the point that I had to block her out of my life. I missed her, but there was so much peace in my life after the relationship ended. God's peace was confirmation that I had been right and that the relationship had needed to end. Since then, God has done so much to heal and deliver my soul. I am free from fear, anxiety, insecurity and rejection. I thank God for my experience with Jessica, because it taught me so much. I love Jessica, and I pray for the blessings of God to cover her life.

Relationships are very important. They direct our destiny. Sometimes you have to remove yourself from a relationship in order to really understand the effects it has on your life. Pay attention to your life. Analyze your motives and the motives of others. Allow God to lead and direct your actions as you move forward.

Affirmations

Say the following affirmations out loud.

- I believe I am receiving God's best.
- My mind is filled with positivity.
- I attract positive people to my life.
- I am good enough.

Take Action

What have you been focusing on?

What do you believe about your life?

You become what's in your mind. What have you been thinking lately?

What do you expect to happen in your life?

What are your character traits, and how do toxic people take advantage of you?

_____

_____

_____

_____

Are you trying to make something work with someone who's not trying at all?

_____

_____

_____

_____

Do you have a friend who connects with your pain but not your purpose? What's holding the relationship together?

_____

_____

_____

_____

_____

CHAPTER 4

————— ☙ ❦ ☙ —————

SEEKING VALIDATION

Is it really love, or are you seeking validation? Is it true friendship, or are you seeking validation? We go through life trying to avoid rejection and denial, and when we experience it, our defense mechanism is to prove our worth in the ways that we know how. When you're in a healthy, loving relationship, you will never need to convince your partner that you're worthy of love and attention. Unfortunately, so many of us are stuck in toxic relationships with partners who show affection and interest sometimes but display emotional distance and a lack of interest most of the time. In this type of relationship, you may internalize that frequent rejection as a sign that you're not good enough. The truth is that, often, the lack of interest your partner is showing in you has nothing to do with you at all.

Often, women who have been victims of infidelity question themselves to determine what they could have done differently to have kept their partners' attention. Many of them believe that if only they were pretty enough, slim enough or fun enough, their partner wouldn't have cheated. The truth is that you *are* enough. There is nothing more you need to do or be to deserve love. You are everything you need to be, and you don't need to change anything about yourself in any attempt to change another person's actions. You can't change them. You can't make them be faithful, and you can't make them be loving or honest. You can't change anyone, and the actions of others have nothing to do with you. Their actions are about them.

An obsessive need to get an emotionally distant partner to notice you, choose you over other women and appreciate you has nothing to do with being in love. The things you do to be accepted and valued are not about love. They are about your deeply rooted need to be validated. You can be deceived into thinking you are chasing and fighting for love, but pursuits like that are all about validation. Think about it. Why chase after someone who ignores you and treats you poorly? That's not how people treat those they love. A healthy relationship involves two people who want to be in it, not one person convincing the other to want to be in it. For some reason, we believe we can change emotionally distant partners' minds and finally prove to them we're worthy of their love.

Your deep roots of insecurity, past rejections and fears are your motivations to continue to fight for validation. Deep down inside, do you know that you struggle to receive validation and acceptance? Maybe your parents raised you to feel invisible or the rejection and pain from past relationships have created deep insecurities in your heart. It's important that you stop hurting yourself by chasing someone who is ignoring you and start working on your healing.

Carrying Spiritual Baggage and Being a People-Pleaser

Some toxic relationships come with spiritual baggage. As you connect with your partner, friend or family member throughout your relationship with them, you may not realize it as it happens, but you begin to carry some of their baggage too. The baggage is draining and weighs you down, but when you finally let go and release the other person, the heavy weight is released. Then, you are able to rebuild your spiritual strength and energy. This is why it's so important to practice saying "no." Other people's spiritual baggage can be overwhelming and stressful, but once you finally release them completely, you will set yourself free.

For years, I was deceived into believing the people who I called my "friends" were actually real friends. Just because you laugh, have fun with a person and enjoy their presence, it doesn't mean it's true friendship. Just because they compliment you and share their toxic life stories freely doesn't make them a friend. It could mean they're lonely and unhappy and need someone who's available to distract them. When they tell you all their toxic secrets, it could only mean that they need to take out the "toxic trash" that they have been holding inside, and because you're a good listener, you are an easy person to dump it on. Because I love helping people and my "friends" often seemed to need it, I would give assistance and advice and become concerned and frustrated when they chose not to follow my direction. I began taking on their issues and mine. It took years for me to stop being a people-pleaser and taking on others' problems that had nothing to do with me.

True friendship can be determined by the actions displayed

during life's challenges. The challenges of life test every relationship, and those who pass the test are those who respond to life's challenges with love, dedication and commitment. Those who fail the test respond by deceiving their "friends" and becoming distant and divisive. Pretenders and fakers enter into relationships solely for their personal benefit. When they are no longer benefiting from the relationship, they walk away. Watch out for these impersonators. They are strong in deceit and have lying spirits. They live their lives in denial as if they're acting in a movie. Other people want to be in your life because they envy you and they want a closer look at what it's like to be you. You should pay attention any time you feel like someone considers you a close friend but you don't feel the same way about them. You may just be allowing them to be around because you're trying to be nice, and you may be ignoring warning signs.

"They smile in your face and all the time they want to take your place...the back stabbers." –The O'Jays

It's important that you analyze your relationships and take your time letting people into your life. True friendship isn't forced, and true love isn't pushy. Watch as life's challenges test your relationships. The Bible warns us to guard our hearts. You should never trust a person who says they love you when they don't love themselves. That's like receiving shelter from a homeless person. How can someone give you what he or she doesn't have?

"Guard your heart above all else, for from it flows the springs of life."-Proverbs 4:23

Your Strongest Beliefs Control Your Life

We aren't perfect. We all have insecurities and weaknesses, but God is always willing to work on our hearts and heal all our brokenness. When you experience mistreatment and invalidation as a child or in relationships as an adult, it affects your belief system and creates lies, such as, "I'm not good enough," "I'm stupid," "I'm ugly," "I'm fat," "I'm a troublemaker," etc. In order for you to heal, it's important that you identify the lies you've been believing about yourself. Realize that these lies are not your fault and that the behaviors you have learned to display in response to them were coping mechanisms you felt like you needed to survive. Know that you do not need them. Understand that you are valuable and worthy of the purpose and life God destined for you to live. God created you in His image, and He loves you.

The invalidation we have receive from people in the past often leads us to seek validation from other people in the present, but validation doesn't come from others. It comes from you. It requires inner work. It's very important that you gain control over your thoughts. Your life is moving in the same direction as your strongest thoughts. Your thoughts become your words, your words become your actions, your actions become your habits and your habits become your character. Finally, your character becomes your destiny. This all starts with your thoughts.

Your thoughts have the power to keep you awake at night, keep you in a state of fear and repetitively torture you. Think about the times when you've become addicted to your thoughts. Maybe they led you to become fearful and obsessively worry. It's important that you understand that you can take control of your thoughts. You don't have to allow negative thoughts to rule your mind. You are the ruler of your mind. It's important that you stop your negative thoughts by denouncing your beliefs in them and replacing them with positive thoughts. Understand this. You are not your emotions.

You may be wondering, "What thoughts should I replace my negative thoughts with?" or "How should I think?" This is how you should think:

"Whatsoever things are true, whatsoever things are honest, whatsoever things are just, whatsoever things are pure, whatsoever things are lovely, whatsoever things are of good report; if there be any virtue, and if there be any praise, think on these things." – Philippians 4:8

You can heal. You can grow and no longer be stuck in the same discouraging mindset. As you complete this healing process, one day you will reach a place in your life where it no longer matters to you what people think about you. You will have zero tolerance for negative thoughts and your own detrimental people-pleasing. Continue to be diligent and faithful and follow God in all that you do to reach that point.

"Be confident of this very thing, that He who has begun a good work in you will complete it until the day of Jesus Christ;"- Philippians 1:6

Affirmations

Say the following affirmations out loud.

- I am validated through my identity in Christ.
- I am more than a conqueror.
- I can do all things through Christ.
- I am healed and my mind is renewed daily.

Take Action

Have you ever chased a person who ignored or mistreated you?

_____

_____

_____

_____

_____

What spiritual baggage have you been carrying from a toxic relationship?

_____

_____

_____

_____

_____

Who has been weighing you down that you are having a hard time releasing?

_____

_____

_____

_____

_____

When did you experience mistreatment and invalidation as a child?

_____

_____

_____

_____

What are the lies you've been believing?

_____

_____

_____

_____

_____

_____

_____

CHAPTER 5

EMOTIONAL ROLLER COASTER

Do people have you on rotate? Is there a pattern in the distances of your relationships? Do you feel like a revolving door as people freely come and go in your life as they see fit? Do you feel like your life is a big waiting room? You're waiting for happiness, love, acceptance, the big proposal and the happy marriage. You're waiting to enjoy your dream of happily ever after. Well, from this moment on you must make the decision to no longer wait. You can live life to the fullest now, and you don't need the permission of another person to do so.

Do you look to others to determine how you feel? If they're happy, you're happy. If they're sad and frustrated, you're anxious and confused. You are living your life on an emotional roller coaster, and it's not fun at all. Any time someone else can control your daily mood or whether or not you're smiling and happy, you have given them emotional control over your life. It's time for you to take back control of your life, and stabilize your emotions and protect your peace. You have to stop allowing people to come and go as they please by creating boundaries, and you must no longer allow people to control your peace of mind.

We often try to fix things and change people. We get emotional and passionate about how they should listen to us and behave properly. Sometimes, the best thing for us to do is be silent. Instead of trying to get them to listen and do what's right, put the situation in God's hands and quiet the storm. The pressures of life can be overwhelming and stressful, but you add to that stress for yourself by loudly trying to be heard, which subconsciously tells yourself and others, "I don't believe my voice is important. I must yell, scream and nag until my volume is loud enough to seem important to your ears." What you fail to realize is that everything about you is enough. You are important enough, and you don't have to try to prove it by trying to get through to people who aren't listening. Silence is a source of great strength. You can confidently rest in the strength of your silence.

For years, I allowed other people's emotions to control my mood, and I got upset when I couldn't fix their problems. I had to understand I can't fix everything and everybody and learn to let things go and rest in my own spiritual mood. I needed to let go and let God. During the first years of my relationship with my husband then boyfriend, we were in college, and in that season in my life, I was very insecure and needy. This personal emotional problem came up for me sometimes when I would meet up with him, feeling energetic and cheerful, and found that he was quiet, calm and observant. I would ask him if anything was wrong and he would always respond, "I'm fine." I couldn't let it go. I always believed something was wrong with him and he just didn't want to tell me.

In my mind, I started thinking that he was holding things back and not being completely honest about his feelings. I became anxious and confused about why he wasn't as energetic and as social as I was. I became uncomfortable and insecure about what was potentially going on with him, but it had nothing to do with me. His mood and feelings were his personally. They had nothing to do with me, but because of my insecurities, I focused on them and allowed them to direct my own feelings. Whether he had something on his mind or not, it wasn't my battle to fight or my baggage to carry, and I had to learn to let it go.

Crying for Love and Attention

My husband and I dated for three years before we got married, and during our years of dating, we went through a season of separation. It started because, during the second year of our relationship, things changed. The first year, he had chased and pursued my heart relentlessly. We talked daily for hours and spent every weekend together from early mornings to late nights. Our relationship was so strong because of our deep connection and friendship. We shared laughs, tears, dreams, goals, secret stories and visions with each other. We grew to know each other on levels that were unknown to others. We couldn't go a day without sharing long intimate conversations with one another. But then came year two.

During this next season of our relationship, our energy changed, and things were different. It was my second year in college and his first year. I was a little more settled into the college life experience, and my expectations were to continue the strong connection of growth in our relationship. Spending quality time and communication is very important to me. It is my love language.

It's a large part of how I receive love. However, my husband, then boyfriend, had different expectations. He expected to spend lots of time meeting and socializing with new people. He still wanted our relationship, but our relationship wasn't on the top of his priority list. He felt that our relationship was strong and solid enough to withstand the new distance that would come with his newly busy social life. He no longer felt the need to spend hours hanging out with me, now that he wanted to explore the college experience.

Unfortunately, Patrick's new excitement for the college experience and my desire to spend quality time with him caused a division in our relationship. I complained that he wasn't making time for me like he did in the past. I cried and practically begged him to make me a priority. Things didn't get better, because Patrick didn't think anything was wrong. He thought that I wasn't appreciative of the short moments we had together in the evenings. He said I wasn't doing much to change things and that I sat around waiting for him to make the change. He felt that I wanted him to sit around with me doing only what I wanted. He felt as if I was trying to control him.

Separating Yourself from Toxic Habits and Emotions

We had no understanding of each other's positions in the situation. I felt the neglect and pain of an emotionally unavailable relationship. I was on an emotional roller coaster, and I needed to free myself. I prayed to God to lead me and Patrick and direct our relationship. After much prayer and consideration, I felt led to take a break from the relationship and allow God to restore us in due time. I needed to let go of the tight grip I had on the relationship. I told Patrick that I wanted to separate for a season and just focus on friendship. I needed to step away to gain control over my emotions and allow God to work on our hearts. Patrick didn't want the separation, but we both realized that it would actually help us to focus more on enhancing our relationship with God and rekindling our strong friendship. It would help us to reevaluate our relationship and confirm what we really wanted.

Our love and friendship grew in that separation. Sometimes you don't miss a good thing until it's gone, and you have to step back it order to really see it for what it is and fully appreciate it. Separation doesn't always feel good, but if you allow God to lead and guide you, you can grow in it. Separation worked in our relationship prior to marriage, and it was through the guidance of prayer and friendship during that separation that led us to a stronger love. We have been happily married for over a decade now, and we've never had to separate in our marriage.

Now, don't get me wrong. Physical separation isn't for every relationship. Physical separation may work to test your relationship prior to marriage, but unless physical, mental or verbal abuse is going on separation is not recommended in a marriage. Sometimes, you may just need to separate yourself from aspects of your relationship. You may need to separate yourself from the complaining, nagging and arguing in your relationship through silence. I recommend that you pray and seek God on how to lead and guide your relationship. The moral of my story is to follow the peace of God. Instead of trying to control the situation and change your partner, release your desires to do so to God. Put your desires in God's hands, and allow Him to do a work of your heart.

I've had seasons in my marriage when my expectations were different from my husband's. I've learned to be less clingy and demanding and to stop trying to force date nights and quality time. Instead, I peacefully communicate my desires to my husband and then let it go and allow God to work on his heart. There were times in our marriage when I complained because I wanted my husband to plan a romantic getaway. My complaints didn't convince him to do so and only led to more arguments and frustrations. One day, I decided to plan something romantic for him instead. Rather than waiting for him to do it, I reserved a suite at a local hotel, scheduled a babysitter for the kids and showed him how much I loved and appreciated him. I didn't wait until it was his birthday or a holiday. This was a "just because" occasion. My motives were to enjoy and celebrate our love. He couldn't stop smiling. This decision to stop nagging him and make the changes I wanted myself worked miracles in our marriage. There are different seasons in marriage, and sometimes couples experience a dry season. It's normal to experience those times, and instead of focusing on what you are lacking from your partner, you can rejuvenate your love by giving the same kind of love, affection and attention you desire. God restores marriages. Ask God to lead you. Put your trust in the Lord.

"For this reason a man will leave his father and mother and be united to his wife, and the two will become one flesh. So they are no longer two, but one flesh. Therefore what God has joined together, let no one separate." –Mark 10: 7-9

"Trust in the Lord will all your heart; and lean not unto your own understanding. In all your ways acknowledge him, and he shall direct your paths." –Proverbs 3:5-6

Endurance in relationships is tougher now than it has ever been. What used to be deep, long conversations are now short text messages. Feelings of insecurities have become natural thoughts, and jealousy is a common daily habit. Trust sometimes seems like an impossible fantasy, and leaving has become the easiest solution. When you experience genuine love and commitment, though, fight for it. You must fight with your prayers, your forgiveness and your unconditional love, because it's worth it. Everybody wants the perfect ending love story, but life isn't the perfect movie from beginning, middle and end. Real life is not a fairy tale. You must be willing to make the best of each moment without knowing the outcome.

We're about to go even deeper. As your life began to transform from your inner being, you will need to apply wisdom and discernment. Discernment is the gift of knowing the unknown. Discernment is a treasure. You'll never be deceived or misled again.

Affirmations

Say the following affirmations out loud.

- I am blessed.
- I accept myself fully.
- I place all my worries in God's hands.
- God is blessing me daily.

- I will make the best of each moment.

Take Action

What relationships have created emotional rollercoasters in your life?

_____

_____

_____

_____

_____

Does your life feel like a big waiting room? Have you been waiting for love, happiness or acceptance?

_____

_____

_____

_____

_____

Do other people control your daily mood?

_____

_____

_____

_____

_____

Do you try hard to fix situations and change people? If so, why?

_____

_____

_____

_____

Is there someone or something that you need to separate yourself from? If so, what's stopping you from letting go?

_____

_____

_____

_____

_____

_____

_____

_____

CHAPTER 6

———————— ❧❦☙❦ ————————

DISCERNING MANIPULATORS (NARCISSISTS, SOCIOPATHS and PSYCHOPATHS)

As you began to heal and God prepares you for growth in your life, you will often be tested. Old friends, past relationships and new relationships similar to past ones will tempt you to fall into weaknesses. If you're not careful you can easily fall into another emotionally unavailable relationship with a manipulative person who can tempt you to ignore what you have learned. but it's important that you gain wisdom and understanding to prevent people from manipulating you into toxic relationships. This is not always easy to recognize when it happens. Everything isn't always what it seems. Even salt looks like sugar. What you see isn't always what you get. Manipulation in a relationship is a gradual deceiving process. Manipulators never start manipulating at the very beginning of the relationship. They take their time to get to know you better and to gain a better understanding of which of your vulnerabilities they can most successfully use to take advantage of you.

There's something about you that's exceptional. You're talented, beautiful, smart and gifted. Manipulators and bullies can see what is amazing in you. They can spot your uniqueness. They can see great things in you that you don't even recognize in yourself. The brilliance and beauty you exemplify is torturing to their insecurity and low self-esteem. It makes them want to passionately and intentionally demean and degrade you. They take on the purpose and calling to do whatever it takes to put you down and block you from being who you were really created to be.

In addition to your gifts, they recognize your lack of self-recognition and your inability to confidently proclaim and assert your true identity, and they attack you where you are weak to make sure that you never get to a place of certainty of and clarity about your radiance. You then become a slave to their abuse, a believer of their words and a prisoner to their torture. As an abused victim, you are left feeling inadequate and insecure. You become broken and bruised from the inside out. You question your worth and your value even more and have an even harder time finding the true essence of your amazing self.

Manipulators Hide Their True Identities

Manipulators are rooted in jealousy, envy and inadequacy. Some manipulators hide their insecurities and weaknesses through arrogance and conceit. They wear a mask of confidence and strength so you cannot tell that they are rooted in emotional fear, anxiety and uncertainty. On the outside, they look strong and certain about life, but on the inside they are broken and confused. The perception of them everyone has is not their real, authentic identity. A manipulator's goal is always to portray the person they want others to see and never break this illusion. Their true identity is hidden, unless it is revealed under pressure. It's the pressures of life that expose the manipulator. This is the very reason why it's so important to take your time and get to know a person before you give your heart to them. Time will reveal a person's habits, and the pressures of life will reveal their character. The reason it's very important to recognize the truth in people and guard your heart in new relationships is because some relationships can cloud your vision and block your blessings as you become more and more embedded in them.

Whether you know it or not, God has a purpose and destiny for your life. When you give your heart to Jesus Christ and invite Him to become Lord over your life, you receive a birthright. You inherit an abundant life. The enemy will use toxic relationships to still, kill and destroy your destiny.

"And those He predestined he also called, and those He called He also justified, those He justified He also glorified." –Romans 8:30

Jesus said, "The thief comes only to steal and kill and destroy. I have come that they may have life, and may have it abundantly."- John 10:10

Discovery Through Discernment

To keep toxic relationships from blocking your blessings, it is important that you use discernment. Discernment is your inner ability to know and see beyond the surface.

Here's an excerpt about discernment from my book, *When*

God Sent My Husband: Wisdoms for Capturing and Keeping a Man's Heart. "We think we know what's best, but we don't. While you're looking at the outer appearance of that man, God knows what is inside his heart. God sees that man twenty years from now, and you are only looking at what he looks like now. He knows that man's temper and how he deals with stress. God sees that man's generational bloodline and the many mental and physical issues that occur from generation to generation.

You only look at how sweet he is toward you during your date and how thoughtful his phone calls and text messages are. You attach your heart to a man you think you know, but God knows the unseen, hidden things of a man's heart. While your heart is focused on marrying someone tall, dark and handsome, God is focused on your spiritual compatibility. Are you equally connected on a spiritual level? When the trials of life come, will the two of you survive? I didn't know that I needed to discern the spirit of a person and be wise as a serpent and harmless as a dove (Matthew 10:16). I didn't know any of these things, and personally, I didn't care. I had a desperate, rebellious spirit, and I was determined to be in a relationship. Instead of me chasing God, I was chasing my idea of love. I idolized having a man."

Discernment comes as you quiet your spirit, listen and pay attention. We often ignore the warning signs of toxic relationships because we're desperate for a sense of love and companionship. Because of our weaknesses of low self-esteem, boredom and loneliness, our minds become intoxicated by any form of acceptance and friendship, and eventually, we are unable to discern the truth even if we ty. This is the reason it's important to nurture and invest in your mind, spirit and soul. When you allow God to fill you and work on your heart, your spirit strengthens and your skills of discernment sharpen.

The main reason we often have trouble discerning the truth is that we would rather believe and accept lies that feel better than the painful truth. If you're in love with a manipulator and abuser, you would rather believe they are always honest and loving to you. It feels better than acknowledging that they are using you and hurting you. Knowing that is painful, and it is easier to settle and believe the lie. The truth sounds like hate to those who hate the truth. Work provides another example for a lot of people. If you're overworked and miserable in a dead-end job, it's easier to ignore the truth that you're settling and choosing to stay because of fear, and it's harder to make a change that you feel insecure and uncertain about. It feels much better to blame the job experience on your coworkers and pay rate, because owning the responsibility for the fact that you aren't consistently seeking other employment to enhance your career is difficult to accept and may make you feel shame. Discernment comes a lot easier when people are willing to accept the truth, no matter how painful it may be. Fear causes us to avoid the truth and live in denial. It's so important that you seek the truth in every area of your life. Jesus said, "If you abide in my word, you are truly my disciples. And you will know the truth, and the truth will set you free." –John 8:31-32 The truth will set you free. It's time you are exposed to the truth about the methods that narcissists, psychopaths and sociopaths use to manipulate you. People who have a narcissistic, psychopathic or sociopathic personality disorder are very manipulative and deceitful. These people often exploit, hurt and demean their loved ones. To avoid taking ownership and responsibility of their faults, they deceive their victims by distorting their sense of reality. The following are a few of the tactics they use.

- Gaslighting is a manipulative strategy to get the victim to question their sanity by telling them, "That didn't happen," "You're crazy" or "You're imagining things." Gaslighting is used to twist your sense of reality. It destroys your ability to trust yourself and paralyzes you from feeling justified in speaking out against abuse and mistreatment. Gaslighting causes you to question whether you can trust your own understanding of what happened. It's very important that you stay grounded in the truth of your reality. Manipulators often implement confusion in arguments to their benefit. Their purpose is to distract you from the main problem by trying to throw you off track and frustrate your own intentions. They may try to make you feel guilty for having thoughts and feelings that are different from their own. Name-calling is a popular tactic that manipulators such as narcissists use when they can't think of a way to change or confuse your opinions or control your emotions. Name-calling is used to keep them above you and to demean and degrade you. Name-calling is a quick and easy way to put you down. The goal is often to insult your appearance, intelligence or values in order to influence you to change your behavior.

It's so important that you slow things down when you find yourself dealing with people who you suspect may be toxic. If you see them speak to or treat another person badly, it's a good chance that one day they may do the same to you. Any terrible treatment they give to someone else will likely translate to their future treatment of you. For example, they may place you on a pedestal while they maliciously degrade their ex. Eventually, once they're comfortable enough with their understanding of your insecurities, they'll start devaluing you. Once they've learned your hidden feelings of inadequacy, they will use that knowledge to provoke you. It's very important that you discern when you're being manipulated so that you can avoid further interaction, engagement and especially entanglement with the manipulator.

You may be wondering how you have better, healthier relationships and live a prosperous life with the people around you. I advise you to remember that the truth will set you free. Stay connected to God, listen for His spiritual guidance, read His word and abide in Him. As you continue to learn the truth, He will set you free from fear, bitterness, abuse, sorrow and pain. As you pursue God's word daily, discernment will guide you. You will start knowing things that aren't obvious in the natural ream. You will began to understand and embrace deeper spiritual knowledge through prayer and revelation.

Affirmations

Say the following affirmations out loud.

- I am talented.
- I am beautiful and smart.
- I am unique and gifted.
- I quiet my spirit and listen to the Holy Spirit daily.
- I accept the truth, and it sets me free.

Take Action

When have you felt uncomfortable showcasing your talents around another person? What made you insecure about expressing your gifts?

_____

_____

_____

_____

_____

What habits will you implement to start taking your time and getting to know person before opening your heart to them?

_____

_____

_____

_____

_____

What emotions are you dealing with that lead to feelings of inadequacy and insecurity?

_____

_____

_____

_____

_____

Have you every moved too fast in a relationship, if so, why?

_____

_____

_____

_____

Have you ever experienced gaslighting? What can you do to prevent someone from trying to manipulate you through gaslighting?

_____

_____

_____

_____

_____

_____

_____

CHAPTER 7

⟪⟫⟪⟫

THE ROOTS OF YOUR HEART CREATE
THE FRUIT OF YOUR LIFE

What's in your heart? What are the roots growing from your inner core that are creating the results of your life? Did you know that your inner emotions are responsible for who you date, who you call your best friend and even how far you go in your career? The roots of your heart are controlling every area of your life. They control whether are not you eat healthy foods and exercise, whether you start a business and whether you get married. The emotions rooted in your heart are powerful. Some of us have roots of fear, doubt and anxiety, even if we also hold onto a little faith and hope.

What were the emotional roots that began growing from your childhood? Did bitterness grow from the pain of a neglectful parent? Did a root of shame and pain sprout up from abuse? Did you start growing the roots of insecurity and low self-esteem after experiencing a toxic relationship?. When you're feeling not good enough, it creates the root of fear of rejection, and this can often lead you to attract disrespect and negativity in relationships. Your feelings of hurt create a root of pain and bitterness that attracts circumstances that will disappoint you further. What you think, you become. If you think you'll never find true love, you will experience the disappointment of toxic love. Your negative emotions will hinder the progression and purpose of your life. They aggressively creating patterns in your mind in order to control your life. The negative emotions many of us deal with daily includes but are not limited to the following.

- worry
- insecurity
- anger
- fear
- depression
- doubt
- inadequacy
- resentment
- shame
- rage
- disappointment
- fatigue
- guilt
- anxiety

Many of us live with those negative emotions daily. Our minds are cluttered with all of those toxic emotions. It's obvious why many of us have a difficult time resting at night and living a life of peace. In today's society, it's very common to take medicine to decrease stress and depression. Our minds, bodies and souls are constantly weighed down by the roots of fear and anxiety. We become so used to these negative emotions that we don't recognize the severe effects they have on our lives.

It's very important that you take action and detoxify yourself from these negative emotions. You must get to the root. To do that, you must first understand where those negative emotions come from. Don't be deceived into thinking God gave them to you. 2 Timothy 1:7 says, "For God has not given us the spirit of fear; but of power, and of love, and of a sound mind." The roots stem from a belief. What lies have you been believing about yourself? Once you discover the root you must come out of agreement with that belief. You must pull the root, terminating the toxic results in your life.

"For the weapons of our warfare are not the weapons of the world. Instead, they have divine power to demolish strongholds. We tear down arguments, and every presumption set up against the knowledge of God; and we take captive every thought into obedience of Christ." –2 Corinthians 10:4-5

Fighting People Hurts You the Most

You destroy your toxic emotional roots through spiritual attacks (such as prayer and meditation), not by hurting others. You can't free yourself through fighting with your ex or saying hateful words to someone who abused you. Remember, your emotional roots are about you, not other people, and they are intangible. It's important that you understand that negative emotions are not physical things, but they are spiritual things that have the power to manifest physical things, and that is why they must be addressed. Everything you see in the physical ream came from a thought in the spiritual ream. We all know a thought can't been physically seen it is first unseen in the spiritual ream. The computer I'm currently typing on came from the thoughts of a computer engineer, the chair I'm sitting in came from the mind of a furniture designer and the home I live in came from the thoughts and creativity of an architect. Your life is a physical manifestation of your thoughts, beliefs, dreams and expectations. Everything you store in the spiritual ream of your mind creates the physically manifested results of your life.

You may be thinking, "But I didn't create the person who mistreated and hurt me." That is true, and sometimes innocent victims are wrongfully mistreated and had nothing to do with their abuser's choices. Each person has a free will and we are not in control of the actions of others. But we are in control of what we allow ourselves to believe, think and expect. This is why two people can both experience the same abuse, neglect and rejection from an abusive relationship but respond differently from each other and experience different results in their lives. One person decides to forgive the person who hurt them, release the pain and live a peaceful, thankful life. The other person decides to hold on to the pain, anger and resentment and live a chaotic, drama-filled life. Although they both had the same painful experiences, both ended up with very different life results because of the individual emotions rooted in them.

This is why it's so important to get rid of the toxic emotional roots in your life. Matthew 3:10 talks about cutting them down and destroying them. "Already now the ax is applied to the root of the trees. Therefore every tree not producing good fruit is cut down and thrown into the fire." Remember that your thoughts create your words, your words create your actions, your actions create your habits and your habits create your character. What's in you comes out. When we are rooted in bitterness and hatred, we produce a life of bitter, hateful fruit, and this fruit is our character. Our character is a reflection of what's inside of us. Do you have trouble controlling you temper? Do you have a tendency to complain and feel ungrateful? It's important to analyze what's rooted in you.

"See to it that no one falls short of the grace of God and that no bitter root grows up to cause trouble and defile many." – Hebrew 12:15

As we think about the importance of cultivating our characters, we must also remember to focus on the characters of others as well. The systems of our world teach us to judge people by the way they look, how much money they have and how others treat them. However, God teaches us not to focus on outward appearance and financial status but to pay attention to their character. Do they display integrity and honesty? Are they kind and loving? Every financially rich person isn't loving and kind and every poor person isn't evil and bitter. On the flip side, every wealthy person isn't greedy and selfish, and every poor person isn't generous and kind-hearted. Whether a person bears good or bad fruit has nothing to do with their bank account, house or career and everything to do with their character.

"You will know them by their fruits. Do men gather grapes from thornbushes or figs from thistles? Even so, every good tree

71

bears good fruit, but a bad tree bears bad fruit. A good tree cannot bear bad fruit, nor can a bad tree bear good fruit." Matthew 7:16-18

Let's consider some examples of negative emotional roots that can rise up and defile the characters of individual people and defile others around them. For example, the bitter roots of jealousy, covetousness, envy and revenge can defile an entire church. Sandy is a member of Faith Baptist church. She's involved in the children's ministry, and she is also a member of the choir. On the outside, Sandy seems to have it all together. She has an amazing career and two beautiful children. She's always smiling and seems happy about life. Most people assume Sandy is a sweet, kind and giving person, but what many don't see is that Sandy is struggling silently. She is really unhappy because her husband left her for another woman. She's lonely and bitter. Sandy dreams of having a life just like Sherry the Pastor's wife. To Sandy, Sherry is the one who seems to have the perfect life. She's married to Pastor Jeff, and her two beautiful children still have a father. Sherry has a prosperous women's ministry, and she is physically beautiful and slim. In her jealousy toward Sherry, Sandy started coveting Sherry's entire life, even her husband, Pastor Jeff. Sandy then became ambitious about pursuing Pastor Jeff by having an affair with him. Unfortunately, Pastor Jeff fell into the temptation and destroyed his marriage by having an ongoing affair with Sandy. Sandy's bitter emotional roots sprung up to destroy the peace and love of the church. Sherry filed for divorce, and as a result of the strife their church and family has been destroyed. Other church members are now defiled with anger, resentment and revenge for the church falling apart. Many of them blame Sandy and Pastor Jeff, and some of them even blame God. As Hebrew 12:15 says, "The bitter root grew up to cause trouble and defile many."

When painful situations like infidelity and divorce occur, we tend to blame people. We become angry and we lash out to get revenge from the people that hurt us. However, that only makes things worse. The anger, pain and bitterness we feel towards others only creates more bitter roots that produces more bad fruit. We waste our time, energy and strength when we focus on hurting and fighting people. The Bible commands us not to fight each other but to fight against spiritual forces of evil by taking on the whole armor of God. This is how you free yourself from the toxic roots in your heart, and this is how you overcome and heal from the painful tragedies of this world. Remember that the emotions you feel and the thoughts you think are spiritual. Therefore, they require spiritual weapons. Read the scriptures below to learn of the spiritual weapons you must use.

"For we do not wrestle against flesh and blood, but against the rulers, against the authorities, against the cosmic powers over this present darkness, against spiritual forces of evil in the heavenly places. Therefore take up the whole armor of God, that you may be able to withstand in the evil day, and having done all to stand firm. Stand firm then, with the belt of truth buckled around your waist, with the breastplate of righteousness in place, and with your feet fitted with readiness that comes from the gospel of peace. In addition to all this, take up the shield of faith, with which you can extinguish all the flaming arrows of the evil one. Take the helmet of salvation and the sword of the Spirit, which is the word of God. And pray in the Spirit on all occasions with all kinds of payers and requests. With this in mind, be alert and always keep on praying for all the Lord's people." –Ephesians 6:12-18

"But put on the Lord Jesus Christ, and make no provision for the flesh, to fulfill its lusts." –Romans 13:14

"Let this mind be in you, which is also in Christ Jesus." – Philippians 2:5

Looking Beyond the Physical Realm

We dig up our negative emotional roots and remove our bitterness, the resentment and the pain through the truth of God's word and the righteousness we have through Christ, whose peace surpasses all understanding. We stand on truth and the knowledge of God as we cover our minds and thoughts with the helmet of salvation. It may seem strange to try to recognize roots of your problems that you cannot see when you're thinking about your problems in the earthly, physical realm, because we are often distracted by our fleshly senses. If we can't physically see it, hear it, feel it, smell it or taste it, we often have a hard time focusing on it, but it is important that we look deeply within ourselves to find our emotional roots.

"While we look not at the things which are seen, but at the things which are not seen. For the things which are seen are temporal, but the things which are not seen are eternal." –2 Corinthians 4:18

You must remove all the bitter roots within you and replace

them with faith and love. Then, your life will manifest the fruits of the Spirit. Always remember that everything the enemy attacks in your life is to get to your faith. You can change your entire life with faith, and you must protect it and fill your heart with it. The Bible says if you have faith the size of a mustard seed, you can move mountains and nothing will be impossible to you (Matthew 17:20).

"But the fruit of the Spirit is love, joy, peace, forbearance, kindness, goodness, faithfulness, gentleness and self-control. Against such things there is no law." –Galatians 5:22-23

Affirmations

Say the following affirmations out loud.

- I trust and have faith in God.
- I give all my worries to God.
- I am peaceful and confident.
- I meditate on God's word day and night.
- I only believe what God says about me.
- I forgive those who hurt me.
- I am grateful.

Take Action

What emotions are rooted in your heart?

_____

_____

_____

_____

_____

What situations or relationships have you encountered that led to fear, doubt or anxiety?

_____

_____

_____

_____

_____

What do you worry about mostly and why?

_____

_____

_____

_____

_____

What lies have you believed about yourself?

_____

_____

_____

_____

_____

What's the hardest thing about forgiving for you?

_____

_____

_____

_____

_____

_____

_____

_____

What are the results you desire in your life, and what are the new habits you need to create in order to manifest those results?

_____

_____

_____

_____

_____

How will you apply the spiritual weapons from Ephesians 6:14-18 in your daily life?

_____

_____

_____

_____

_____

_____

❧☙❦❧

DIVINE SECRET TO LIVE AN ABUNDA

Let's get right down to it. The divine secret to living an abundant life starts in your mind. If you change your mind, you'll change your life. "For as he thinks in his heart, so is he." –Proverbs 23:7

However, in order to change your mind, it's very important that you understand the power of your subconscious mind. Your subconscious mind is where all your power is held. It's much more powerful than your conscious mind. Your subconscious mind is an unlimited memory bank that permanently stores everything that has ever happened to you. The job of your subconscious mind is to take all the data from your life's experiences and program in you the beliefs, understandings and interpretations to help you respond to new experiences according to the old ones. Your subconscious mind is a pattern machine that operates in a system that was established by your past. In other words, your past experiences influence your present reactions through your subconscious mind. Everything you believe, say and do is a reflection of the pattern and programming of your subconscious mind.

This is the very reason why, whenever you attempt something new, your subconscious mind will try to pull you back into the pattern and programming of your comfort zones. Your comfort zones are what come naturally to you. You believe, think and do everything that is in your comfort zone without much effort or ssure. These comfortable beliefs, thoughts and actions flow naturally through you. Understand that your subconscious mind is the automatic program function of your life, and it's very important to always be aware of the kind of thoughts and actions that feel natural to you and how they affect your life. We can transform our lives by paying attention to our subconscious programming and working to change and renew it. This is why the Bible tells us to be transformed by the renewing of our minds (Romans 12:2).

Your subconscious mind also doesn't know the difference between real situations and visualizations. This is why you scream and become really scared while watching horror movies, and why you get really excited when thinking about your goals and dreams. Your subconscious mind thinks that what you are watching or planning is what you are experiencing. This is why it's very important to guard what you see and hear, because what you see and hear gets into your subconscious mind just as much as what you actively choose to experience. You must also be careful because the longer your subconscious mind believes something, the harder it is to change that belief

What You Expect Becomes Your Reality
Remember that every thought becomes a physical reaction, every emotional root comes through in your character and every experience affects your subconscious, influencing your thoughts. Sometimes, when your thoughts, emotional roots or past experiences are negative, all of these truths can feel like a vicious cycle that conspire against you. The good news is that, by the

power of Jesus Christ all things are possible, and even the hardest changes can come more quickly than you expect. Guard your mind from all doubt and defeat, because what you expect often becomes your reality. Focus on God instead.

We all have a body, a spirit and a soul made up of our mind, emotions, conscience and will. However, the moment you invite Christ to be Lord over your life, you become a new creature.

"Therefore if anyone is in Christ, he is a new creation. The old has passed away; behold, the new has come." -2 Corinthians 5:17

When your spirit finds a connection with God, you gain the power to communicate with Him and hear His voice. The Holy Spirit begins renewing you from the inside out. Through prayer and connecting with God by studying His word, you open yourself up for God to reprogram your emotions, mind and will until they all lines up with His calling and purpose for your life. This is why it's important to spend quiet time listening for God's word and seeking the direction of the Holy Spirit.

Years ago, when I was a young wife, whenever my husband and I got into big arguments and disagreements, my stubborn, selfish conscience wanted to take over. I would be so mad at my husband over petty stuff that I would contemplate leaving him. The Holy Spirit would speak really softly to me and tell me to apologize. My stubborn personality would question God, saying, "Why should I apologize? He was wrong, and I deserve an apology from him." In my adult life, I had overcome my childhood feelings of inadequacy, and my more recent life experiences and personal opinions had shaped my conscience to give up on anything that didn't serve me or make me happy. The Holy Spirit awakened my conscience and guided my actions in the direction of God's purpose for my life. God taught me how to humble myself and forgive quickly. The more I followed the guidance of the Holy Spirit and apologized first, the easier it became to work out our marriage disagreements. God often connects with us through our spirit and soul. This is the reason why, when God speaks to you, it often feels like an inner knowing or intuition. It's because he comes through you from your core, your heart and your inner spirit.

God wants you to understand the will and calling on your life. It's time for you to become enlightened in your understanding so that you have no more confusion or uncertainty about the life of abundance he has in store for you.

"The eyes of your understanding being enlightened; that you may know what is the hope of his calling, and what the riches of the glory of his inheritance in the saints." –Ephesians 1:18

Transform Your Mind Through Meditation

If you are ready to reprogram your mind to start living an abundant life and fulfilling your destiny, plan a good length of quiet time to sit down and follow the steps listed below.

1) Figure out exactly what you desire for your life according to God's will. You may desire a healthy marriage, healing in your mind or body or a financial breakthrough. Whatever it is, write it down below.

_____

_____

_____

_____

2) Write out a scripture from the Bible that supports God's will for you to have what you desire. For instance, if you desire healing, you might write down, "For I will restore health to you and heal you of your wounds." From Jeremiah 30:17. If you desire a healthy marriage, you might choose, "Therefore what God has joined together, let not man separate." –Matthew 19:6. If you're having trouble finding a scripture, go to google.com and search the words, "scripture on _____," filling the blank with whatever your desire is. Write the scripture that you choose below.

_____

_____

_____

_____

3) Expose the negative doubts and thoughts that are hindering you from believing in and receiving your blessing. Write down every thought or fear that's preventing you from receiving God's will for your life.

_____

_____

_____

_____

4) Visualize how it would feel to receive the blessing you desire. Imagine that you are receiving it, and then pay attention to how you feel when it comes. What does your blessing look like? Describe the environment you see around you in the vision. How do you feel moments after receiving your blessing? Days? Months? Write it all out.

_____

_____

_____

_____

5) Write out the way your everyday life looks and feels after you have received your blessing.

_____

_____

_____

_____

_____

_____

_____

6) Relive a moment when you felt like you were on top of the world. Then write out your experience of that moment of excitement and joy.

_____

_____

_____

_____

_____

_____

_____

7) Now, it's time to meditate. Read over your writings from 1-3 and meditate on them through prayer, thanksgiving and acknowledgment to God. I recommend that you also record your prayers. Most cell phones have a voice memo app that allows you to record messages. When you have thoughtfully prayed to God, then quickly reread numbers 4-5, letting the images and visualization mix in your mind. Finally, read number 6 and end your mediation in prayer and worship to God for all you have already received. This method has changed my life tremendously. It has set me free from anxiety, fear and sickness. I pray that this will bless and transform your mind and that the mind of Christ will also be in you (Philippians 2:5).

CHAPTER 9

BEING ENOUGH

Now that you know the truth that you are enough, it's time to live it. Walk, speak and function in the truth of being enough.

"Before I formed you in the womb I knew you." –Jeremiah 1:5

It's very important that you understand that before you were formed in the womb of your mother, before you were born into this world, before you were named, God knew you. To know someone is to be aware of them through observation, information and relationship. You come to know someone by spending time with them and becoming familiar with their nuances. Therefore, before you were mistreated, neglected, used, abused and rejected in this world, the Almighty God knew the essence of your spirit and soul. You are not who people call you, you are not the titles you've earned from education and careers and you are not the relationship status title on your social media page. You are so much more.

Your problems begun when you allowed the pressures of life and the pain of disappointment to define you and tell you that you weren't enough. If only you had meditated then on the fact that God knew you and called you before He formed you into your physical self, you would be walking right now in the grace and confidence of being enough. It's time for you to make the conscious decision to never again allow a person or situation to stop you from being the person you're meant to be. God said, "You are fearfully and wonderfully made (Psalm 139:14)" and "Let us make man in our image after our likeness. (Genesis 1:26)."

Believe, Think and Speak Positive Affirmations

It's helpful for you to meditate on the fact that God made you to be enough and speak positive affirmations over your life. Say the follow affirmations out loud daily before bedtime and early in the morning.

- I can do all things through Christ who strengthens me. (Philippians 4:13)
- Abundance flows in and through me daily.
- My thoughts are filled with positivity, and my life is plentiful with prosperity.
- I am surrounded by positive, genuine people.
- My God shall supply all my need according to His riches in glory by Christ Jesus. (Philippians 4:19)
- Jesus keeps me in perfect peace, as my mind is stayed on Him, because I trust in Him (Isaiah 26:3)

Affirmations are important because they are declarations of what you believe, expect and desire to manifest in your life. Whether you understand it or not, your words are powerful. You have the power to speak life or death into existence. You have the power to speak victory or defeat into your marriage, family, career or business. What you speak over your life brings forth results. When you affirm positive words of hope, you are planting seeds of prosperity in your life and directing your decisions and habits towards the optimistic outcomes you desire.

"Death and life are in the power of the tongue and they that love it shall eat the fruit thereof." –Proverbs 18:21

In order to live a life of someone who knows they are enough, you must stop comparing yourself to others. It's very easy to compare yourself to others without even realizing it. With social media and reality TV, we are constantly exposed to the real-life experiences of celebrities, old classmates, neighbors and even coworkers, and comparing small and large details of your life experiences to another person is very tempting. Whether we compare our weaknesses to others' strengths or feel prideful about our strengths while looking down on others' weaknesses, both are very unfair. We are all uniquely created and specifically called to an individual purpose, and comparison to others is not useful to God's calling for us.

God has specific things He wants to do in specific seasons in your life. It's up to you to jump on board and go where God leads you. He will never force it. You have to be willing to stay focused on Him. When we become distracted and consumed by other peoples' lives, we miss what God is trying to do in our own lives. Maybe you are so focused on how she lost the weight that you can't figure out why you can't lose a pound. Maybe you can't understand why he married her and didn't marry you or why your sister has a bigger house than yours. Those thoughts are cancerous to the joy and peace of your life. The comparisons won't allow you to rest in the contentment of being enough. Those thoughts give rise to feelings of not being enough that spread to other areas of your life as well. At times, our thoughts are filled with so much insecurity that they create lies that we start believe. This is why it's so important to focus on, speak and believe the word of God. God tells us, "You lack no good thing." (Psalm 34:10) You lack nothing, and you are enough.

Stay in Your Lane

A few years ago, I struggled with comparing the successes of other ministries and authors to the work that God was doing in my life. I would compare the number of others' social media fans and book sales to my own. God would softly tell me to stop focusing on the numbers, but the comparison started taking up my time. Instead of focusing on my own plans and assignments, I was spending hours researching, reading and reviewing their projects. I would make excuses that I was learning from my peers and staying connected, but really, I had the wrong motives.

One morning, during my journaling time, I heard God speak to me, saying, "Rainie, you can easily become distracted by following and watching what others are doing. But I've called you to something different. Nothing I call you to will be forced. It will flow and be purposeful. It will have meaning and purpose. You won't have time to see what others are doing in their ministries, because you will be too focused on yours. Rainie, stay committed to the work you have to complete. It's going to help heal you to know you are enough." After I received that message from God, I felt led to stop following the people I was comparing myself to on social media and start committing to my work and God's calling for my life. I became more disciplined in my daily assignments and focused on my own strategies, goals and accomplishments. Today, I live by the slogan, "I am staying in my lane." I've decided to embrace my calling and stay in the lane God has prepared before me. I no longer covet others' successes, but I rejoice in their victories and joyfully maintain mine with gratitude.

The following is an excerpt from my book, *Undeniable Breakthrough*. "The key is to get your mind off the gradual progress. Be thankful and appreciate your small improvements, but do not focus on them. Your focus must stay on consistently and diligently trusting that, as you work on the plan, you will reap results. It may take months, years or even decades to complete, but God's grace is sufficient, and regardless of what you are working towards, He will strengthen you to do all things. Remember Philippians 4:13: 'I can do all things through Christ who strengthens me.'

This is why it's important that God strengthen your character, patience and endurance. If you're not properly prepared for your breakthrough, your breakthrough might break you.

In the book *Can You Stand To Be Blessed*, Bishop T.D. Jakes describes how he prayed that God would move mightily in his ministry. The Lord answered him by saying, "You are concerned about building a ministry, but I'm concerned about building a man." Then God said, "Woe unto the man whose ministry becomes bigger than he is!" God will never give you more than you can handle. He allows you to grow gradually because he loves you and He would never want His blessings to overwhelm and harm you. When you're not well prepared, too much of anything can become harmful. But when God sees you being faithful and accepting the gradual increases He grants you, He will trust you with more."

Sometimes its difficult to see yourself as enough when you're dealing with your flaws, insecurities and weaknesses. However, when you start seeing yourself as God sees you, you will recognize the greatness inside of you. In the beginning, it can be difficult to receive all the things God says about you, like, "you are more than a conqueror and you can do all things through Christ," because they seem too generous and feel like things you don't deserve. God's word says you're blessed and highly favored but you may not feel or look blessed. This is the reason it's important not to focus on your current situation but to open yourself up for God to change it. God will bring life to every dead situation and speak into existence things that don't exist. You have to look beyond where you are today and talk, walk, dress, work and be as you desire.

"God gives life to the dead and calls those things that be not as though they were." –Romans 4:17

There have been times when I felt weak and broken in my spirit, and God would tell me that I'm a giant in spirit. I started speaking it over my life as an affirmation and living it as if I felt it were true, and eventually I became it. I recently went through so much turmoil that, if I had gone through the same adversity a few months earlier, I would have been hospitalized. Fortunately, I know how to strengthen myself from the inside out by praying, fasting, meditating and speaking affirmations to ease my mind. I rose out of the trap that was sent by the enemy to hinder my growth, and now I'm stronger and wiser than ever before. I endured the breaking point that was meant to defeat me, and now I'm walking into my breakthrough.

Regardless of what's going on in your relationships right now, whether they're emotionally unavailable or toxic, you no longer have to be bound by another person. If your significant other often initiates fights and drags you down with complaints, it's time that you set yourself free from their drama. This requires you to determine that you will no longer feed into their feuds. You can no longer allow their hostility to take up your precious, valuable time. Choose to remove yourself from any toxic environments and to be silent in the face of smaller toxic behaviors by the ones you love. It's important to protect your peace and allow the Holy Spirit to guide you. Remember that you are enough and you no longer need to try to gain validation or approval from anyone. Stand in the power and victory that's given through Jesus Christ and keep shining your light. Whenever people try to dim your light, that's a sign that they can't handle your brightness, and that's okay. You just go and shine it where it's appreciated and keep being enough.

Affirmations

Say the following affirmations out loud.

- I am enough.
- God knew me before He formed me in the womb.
- I am fearfully and wonderfully made.
- I am made in the image of God.

- My words are powerful.
- I am confident in being myself.
- I am staying in the lane God has prepared for me.

Take Action

What's stopping you from believing that you are enough?

_____

_____

_____

_____

_____

Analyze your words. What do you speak into your life?

_____

_____

_____

_____

Who do you compare yourself to and why?

_____

_____

_____

_____

_____

What daily habits will you implement to help yourself stop being discouraged by your current situation?

_____

_____

_____

_____

_____

_____

CONCLUSION

Often, you'll be presented with the same thing in a different package to see whether you've learned anything. Maybe you end a toxic relationship, and another one comes to you later in a different form. It's the same type of emotionally unavailable relationship with a different name and story. Pay attention to familiarity in people and opportunities, and don't be fooled into opening your heart to a new heartbreaker.

This book was written to change your life and help you create new habits. If you read this book quickly, go back through it again and meditate on the principals and advice so that it becomes embedded in you. Write out all the answers to the questions in each chapter to discover more about yourself. Once you're tested again later in life with the same situation in a different package, you'll make wiser decisions.

Remember to always be a reflection of what you desire to receive. If you want love, give love. If you want truth and honesty, be truthful and honest. What you give will always come back. Be watchful of fake friendship. People aren't your real friends if they never ask how you're doing. If your conversations are usually about them and they're never concerned about how you're doing, that's a sign that your wellbeing isn't genuinely important to them.

Finally, it's so important that you learn how to be a friend to yourself. As you continue to invest in your growth in that direction, you will keep reaping the blessings of it. You no longer have to lose yourself in other people. You can love God and love who God created you to be, and you will never need to seek validation from anyone else, because you are enough!

Now I would like to ask you to do me a favor. Please share your review of this book online wherever you ordered it. I also want to connect with you and hear about your story. Send me a testimony of how this book has blessed your life along with a selfie of you with the book, including #RainieHoward and #YouAreEnough through social media @RainieHoward.

You can also find free resources and connect with me through my website, www.RainieHoward.com.

ABOUT THE AUTHOR

Rainie Howard is a wife, mother and mentor. She has authored several books, including *Addicted To Pain*. She is a sought-after speaker and founder of Sisters of Hope, an organization that promotes women's empowerment. Rainie's mission is to share the love of Christ with people who are hurting all over the world. She and her husband, Patrick Howard, are the founders of "RealLoveExist," a movement that promotes real love stories and healthy relationships, encouraging others to never give up on love.

To learn more, go to www.RealLoveExist.com.

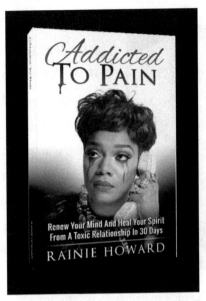

ARE YOU ADDICTED TO A TOXIC LOVE?

The obsession of a toxic relationship can have the same enticement as drugs or alcohol. The pattern echoes time and time again: a new significant other draws you into a new relationship that starts off loving and alluring only to develop into a hurtful or abusive cycle. It's an unhealthy view on love that will rationalize toxic behavior and make another person cling to a relationship long after it should have ended.

A person with a healthy understanding of "true love" will not tolerate this kind of pain. He or she will move on in search of a healthier bond. Like any other addiction, those hooked on toxic love have little or no control over excessive urges to text, call, manipulate or beg for love, attention and affection. They want help. They want to end the pain and recover, but it's just like trying to shake a drug habit. Get your copy at http://bit.ly/AddictedToPain.

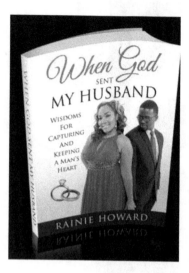

HAVE YOU BEEN PRAYING FOR A HUSBAND?

It's not easy being single, and when you have a vision to be married, it's challenging to patiently wait for the right man. It's important to understand that God has a divine purpose for your life and that He wants to gift you with the right man. *When God Sent My Husband* is a single women's guide to gaining wisdom on:

- How to guard your heart yet freely love
- Preparing and positioning yourself to receive love
- Building a solid foundation that captures and keeps love

In this book, Rainie Howard shares her personal story of seeking love, dating and embracing the divine experience of God bringing her husband into her life. This is a miraculous story of God being the ultimate matchmaker. The book will encourage you to take a spiritual approach towards dating and preparing for marriage. Get your copy at http://bit.ly/WhenGodSentMyHusband.

EVER FELT STUCK OR WEIGHED DOWN BY THE PRESSURES OF LIFE? No matter how hard you try, you just can't get unstuck. It's like sitting in a car, pushing down on the accelerator as hard as you can and the car never moving. You are running in the race of life, but you're getting nowhere. Doors are constantly closing, opportunities are nowhere to be found and you can't get your breakthrough. You've tried everything, but nothing seems to work. You are in desperate need of an "Undeniable Breakthrough!" Whether you need a breakthrough in your relationship, career, finances or health, this spiritual guide will give you all the life strategies you need to experience the blessings of an undeniable breakthrough. Get your copy at http://bit.ly/UndeniableBreakthrough.

CPSIA information can be obtained
at www.ICGtesting.com
Printed in the USA
FSHW011424220520

9 781734 015522